Easy-to-Make

Statement Jewelry

BOLD NECKLACES TO DRESS UP OR DRESS DOWN

Easy-to-Make

Statement Jewelry

BOLD NECKLACES TO DRESS UP OR DRESS DOWN

DESIGN ORIGINALS
an Imprint of Fox Chapel Publishing
www.d-originals.com

We would like to acknowledge the extremely talented creative team at Cousin Corporation of America for their contributions to this book. A special thanks to Kristine Regan Daniel, Jennifer Eno-Wolf, and Chloe Pemberton for their additional support.

Acquisition editor: Peg Couch
Cover and page designers: Llara Pazdan & Justin Speers
Layout designer: Wendy Reynolds
Editors: Colleen Dorsey & Katie Weeber
Technical editor: Melissa Younger
Copy editor: Laura Taylor
Photography: Mike Mihalo
Photography styling: Llara Pazdan, Kati Erney & Kate Lanphier

ISBN 978-1-4972-0313-6

© 2017 by Cousin Corporation of America and New Design Originals Corporation, *www.d-originals.com*, an imprint of Fox Chapel Publishing, 800-457-9112, 1970 Broad Street, East Petersburg, PA 17520.

Library of Congress Cataloging-in-Publication Control Number : 2017006736

Printed in the United States of America
First printing

You Can DIY This!

Jewelry making should be simple, right? Find some fabulous focal beads, connect them to a chain, attach a clasp, and you're ready to go! But when you sit down to make a project, you might feel overwhelmed by all of the techniques and vocabulary. What is the difference between a briolette and a rondelle, and how exactly do you assemble a dramatic statement necklace? Don't be intimidated—this book is specifically designed to break it all down and keep things simple so you can unleash your creativity without fear. You'll build a foundation first, learning the basic vocabulary and techniques so you'll feel totally confident when you sit down to tackle your first project.

Diving into your first project means a trip to the craft store to gather your supplies. Shopping the jewelry aisle can be intimidating. There is always a vast array of options on display, and you don't want to arrive home to discover you missed an essential component. To keep your shopping trips straightforward and simple, each project includes a shopping list you can take to the store with you. Throw this book in your bag, or use your phone to snap a photo of the list so you are never in doubt about what you need.

Once you've made a few projects, you might get the DIY itch to make a few tweaks. And you should! That's the point of making your own jewelry, right? Instructions are provided for each project so you can reproduce the design exactly as you see it, but you should never hesitate to get creative and change it up. Each of us has a unique style, favorite color palette, and favorite outfit. If a design uses suede cord and you prefer ribbon, don't be afraid to make it with ribbon! The same goes for bead color and shape. If you see something that makes a statement in the beading aisle, go ahead and use it!

This book sets you up with all of the tools you'll need to master DIY jewelry making. With a touch of your unique style and creativity, you can make these projects your own. It's time to dive in and get started!

Happy crafting!

Contents

Deco Fringe Necklace

Vintage Charm Necklace

Desert Blues Drop
Necklace

Noir Rope Necklace

Aztec Bib Necklace

Turquoise Rose Necklace

Rainbow Crystal Necklace

Violet Medallion Necklace

40

Chandelier Necklace

42

Edgy Angles Gem
Necklace

44

Ombré Fringe Necklace

46

Chunky Stone Necklace

48

Black Pearl Treasure
Necklace

50

Out on the Town Necklace

52

Golden Fan Necklace

54

Spiked Scarf Necklace

56

Rose Drop Necklace

58

Beaded Stalactite Necklace

60

Beaded Collar
Necklace Set

62

Sienna Gold Necklace

Getting Started

If you are totally new to jewelry making, this is the place to start. This section will help you build a foundation by allowing you to familiarize yourself with the common tools and materials used in jewelry making. You'll also find step-by-step tutorials for the techniques you'll need to assemble the projects in this book. When you're finished, you'll be able to spot filigree connectors when shopping at the craft store and be able to fashion head pins and eye pins into stunning bead drops and links. Once you have a grasp of the content in this section, you'll be ready to tackle your first jewelry project!

Tools

You don't need to spend a lot of money purchasing a vast array of tools to get started with jewelry making. A few sets of pliers and a handful of extras will allow you to make all of the projects in this book. Here are the common tools of jewelry making.

A

B

C

D

THE ESSENTIALS

Needle-nose pliers (A) come to a tapered point, making them the perfect tool to get into small areas of a jewelry design. Use this tool to hold small pieces, open and close jump rings, and manipulate wire.

Round-nose pliers (B) have rounded prongs that are used for making loops in wire, head pins, or eye pins.

Crimping pliers (C) are pliers made specifically for use with crimp tubes. The specially shaped grooves in these pliers will attach a crimp tube to beading wire in the most secure way possible.

Wire cutters (D) should always be used to cut jewelry wire—do not use scissors. Regular wire cutters that you get from the hardware store will work, but flush cutters made specifically for jewelry making are recommended.

THE EXTRAS

Memory wire cutters are heavy-duty wire cutters made specifically to cut the coils of memory wire without affecting their shape.

E-6000® glue is an extra-strong craft glue. It is perfect for securing cord ends or connecting other components.

A *jewelry hammer* is a lightweight hammer used for shaping metal. This hammer has two heads—a flat head and a round head.

A *ring mandrel* is a tapered rod used to measure the size of a ring or, in the case of jewelry making, to shape a ring to a specific size.

Beading tweezers are helpful when it comes to sorting and handling beads. Their extra-fine tip means they can pick up tiny beads more easily than your fingers can. Some tweezers come with a small, spoon-like scoop on the back end for easily collecting loose beads.

A *bead reamer* is like a mini drill that comes with an assortment of tips, which are used like drill bits. The tips can clean up the edges of a hole drilled in a bead, straighten the hole, or otherwise enlarge or re-shape the hole.

Awls are sharp, pointed tools used for making holes in leather.

TOOLS & MATERIALS

Beads

Of course beads are needed for jewelry making, but you might be surprised by the vast number of shapes and sizes that are available. What is the difference between a rondelle and a briolette? Take a look at this collection of commonly used beads to learn some important terms.

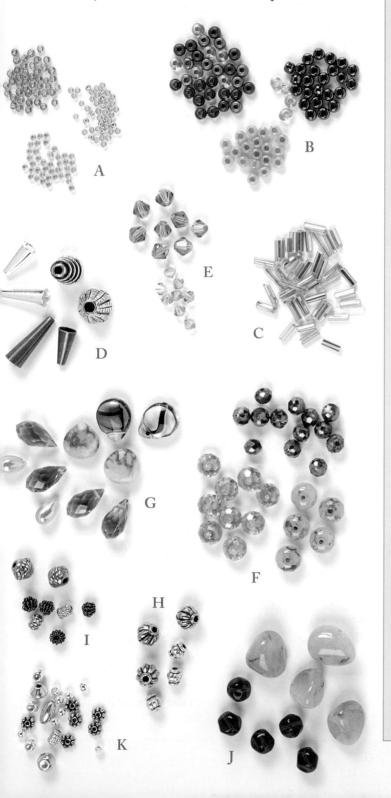

Seed beads (A) are extra-small beads, ranging in size from about 1.5mm to 3mm. Their sizes are listed as a number over zero (15/0, 12/0, etc.). The smaller the initial number, the larger the bead.

E-beads (B) are large seed beads, size 6/0, or about 4mm.

Bugle beads (C) are small, tube-shaped beads.

Cones (D) have a cone shape with a wide base at one end and a tapered point at the other. They are hollow, so they can fit over small components in a design.

Bicones (E) look like two cones that have been joined at the bottom. In profile, they have a diamond shape, with the widest point across the center and a tapered point at each end.

Rondelles (F) look like round, spherical beads that have been squashed just slightly. They look a bit like inner tubes.

Briolettes (G) have a teardrop or pear shape. They are almost always faceted (cut to have multiple faces, like a diamond) and always side-drilled, with a hole through the tapered point of the bead, rather than through the center of the bead.

Melon beads (H) actually have a pumpkin-like appearance, with raised, rounded sections running from top to bottom.

Beehive beads (I) are shaped like beehives you might see in cartoons with raised, rounded sections like rings running around the circumference of the bead.

Nuggets (J) have no specific shape. They are like pebbles you might pick up on the beach—random and unique.

Spacer beads (K) refer to small, plain, typically metallic beads. These beads serve an important function by adding space to a jewelry design without detracting from the focal beads.

Stringing Materials

Stringing materials include all of the items you can string beads onto or attach beads to. Stringing materials like cotton rope or hemp cord can also be used without beads to create jewelry using decorative knotwork. Here is a collection of common stringing materials.

Beading wire (A) is made from several thin wires twisted together and coated with a thin layer of nylon, making it very strong but also very flexible. The more strands used to make the wire, the more flexible it will be. It is used for stringing beads.

Gauge wire (B) is a single piece of metal measured by the thickness of its diameter (gauge). The smaller the gauge number, the thicker the wire is. Gauge wire has varying flexibility and can be used for stringing beads, wire wrapping, or creating fixed components in a design.

Memory wire (C) is gauge wire that has been shaped into coils. The coils can be cut or stretched, but cannot be used for wrapping or other decorative wire work.

Cord (D) generally encompasses any non-wire material used for stringing beads. It is typically made of fabric, fiber, or natural materials. Cording includes satin, leather or suede, rope, or hemp.

Monofilament (E) is an often transparent synthetic cord, similar to fishing line. It is available in different strengths based on the amount of weight it can hold (2 lb. monofilament can hold two pounds of beads).

Chain (F) is a series of metal links joined together. The links may be closed (solid pieces of metal) or open (with a slit cut through them so they can be opened and removed from the main chain). Chain is available in a variety of shapes—cable, curb, and flat-link are the types you'll encounter the most in this book. (For more about different kinds of chain, see the glossary.)

Findings

Findings are all of the components used to build a piece of jewelry. They attach, link, and hold together all of the elements in a design. Here is a collection of common jewelry findings.

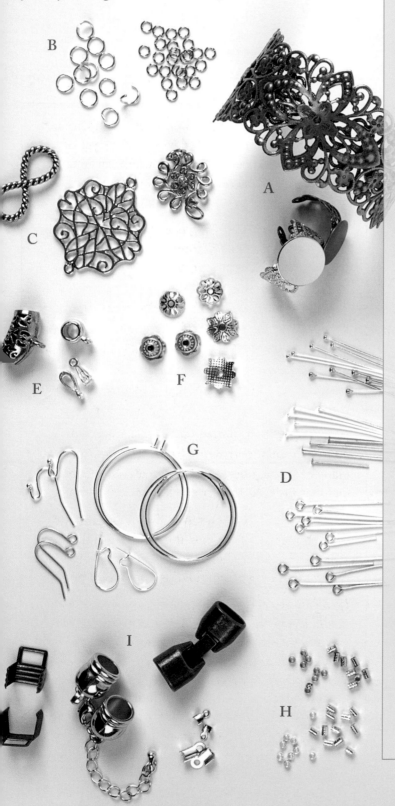

Bases (A) are unembellished blanks that you build upon to create a jewelry piece, such as a ring blank or a bangle bracelet blank.

Jump rings (B) are the most commonly used component to connect different pieces in a jewelry design. They are almost always "open" with a slit cut into the ring so it can be opened and closed. They are also available as solid rings, called closed jump rings.

Connectors (C) are bars, beads, or other components that have a loop (or loops) on each end. They are used to connect separate elements in a design.

Head pins, *ball head pins*, and *eye pins (D)* are short lengths of wire finished at one end with a flat head (head pin), ball (ball head pin), or loop (eye pin). Beads are strung onto the pins and the ends are formed into loops to create decorative bead drops or links.

Bails (E) are used to attach pendants to chain, cord, wire, or other stringing materials.

Bead caps (F) are bowl-shaped decorative components paired with beads. Their shape allows them to fit snugly against the bead as if they were part of it rather than a separate element.

Earring wires (G) encompass any component used to hook an earring to the ear. They come in a variety of shapes including hooks (also known as earring wires or French hooks), kidney wires, and hoops.

Crimp tubes and *crimp beads (H)* are used to finish the ends of beading wire.

Cord ends (I) are used to finish the ends of cord designs without knots. They come as caps that slide over the cord ends and are secured with glue, or crimps, which are clamped onto the cord ends.

Clasps (J, at top) are placed at the ends of a design and are used to close it. They come in numerous shapes and sizes including lobster clasps, toggle sets, or magnetic clasps.

Opening and Closing Jump Rings

Jump rings are used to connect different jewelry components to one another. Opening and closing a jump ring incorrectly can affect its shape or leave gaps that might allow jewelry components to fall off, so it's important to know how to do it properly.

Project(s) using this technique appear on pages 24, 26, 28, 32, 36, 38, 40, 42, 44, 46, 48, 50, 52, 54, 56, 58, and 62.

1   *Position the pliers.* It is best to use two needle-nose pliers for this process. Using the pliers, grasp the ring on each side of the opening.

2   *Start twisting the ring open.* To keep the ring's shape, it should be twisted open, with the ends moving back to front instead of side to side. To do this, twist one wrist toward your body and the other wrist away from your body.

3   *Finish opening the ring.* Continue twisting until the opening is wide enough to attach the desired components. String on components like chain, clasps, or bead drops.

4   *Close the ring.* Following the method in Steps 1–3, reposition the pliers and twist the ring closed. If there is a gap, gently wiggle the pliers, moving the ends of the ring backward and forward while gently pressing them together. The ends should slightly overlap and then snap together tightly so the tension of the metal will hold the ring closed.

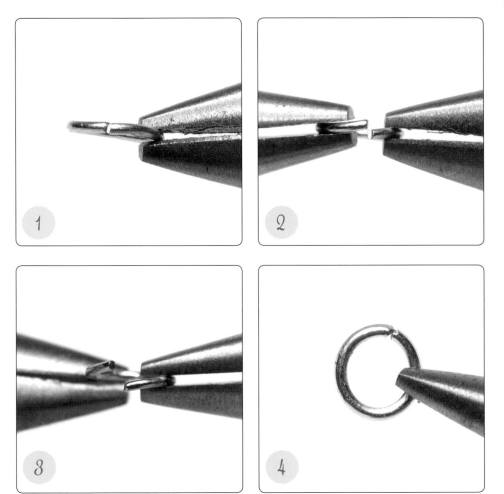

Split rings are like miniature key rings. They are made of coiled wire and do not have openings like jump rings, making them a more secure and sturdy option for heavy components. To attach items to a split ring, use a head pin or eye pin to hold the coils open.

Attaching Crimp Tubes/Beads

Crimp tubes and beads are used with beading wire and secured using crimping pliers. Once crimped, the tubes/beads stay in place on the wire, so they can be used to attach clasps or hold individual beads or groups of beads in a certain place.

Project(s) using this technique appear on pages 34, 36, 38, 42, 48, 52, 56, 60, and 62.

1 **String the clasp.** String a crimp tube and a clasp (such as one half of a toggle clasp or a single lobster clasp) onto a strand of beading wire. Bring the end of the wire back through the crimp tube, creating a ½" (1.3cm) tail. Push the crimp tube up the wire so it is close to the clasp.

2 **Make the first crimp.** Place the crimp tube in the U-shaped groove of the crimping pliers (closest to the handles). Separate the wires in the crimp tube so they are parallel and do not cross. Firmly collapse the crimp tube, forming it into a U shape with one wire in each groove.

3 **Make the second crimp.** Place the crimp tube in the oval-shaped groove of the crimping pliers (farthest from the handles). Position the crimp tube so the U shape is sideways. Squeeze the pliers so the ends of the U shape come together.

4 **Check the wire.** Once crimped, the tube will look like this. Tug on the wire to be sure it is secure. The tail of the wire can be hidden in beads strung onto the wire.

Crimp beads (below right) can be shaped using the crimp tube method described above. They are formed into smooth cylinders using the oval-shaped groove of the crimping pliers, or simply flattened using needle-nose pliers.

Cutting Chain

Jewelry projects often require lengths of chain that are shorter than what you can purchase. Use wire cutters to cut closed-link chain to the length needed. This method allows you to easily cut multiple pieces of chain to the same length without measuring each piece.

Project(s) using this technique appear on pages 24, 26, 28, 32, 40, 42, 44, 46, 50, 52, 54, 56, 58, and 62.

1 **Cut the first length.** Measure the length of chain needed and use wire cutters to cut it off the original chain. Remember, the cut link will fall off, so do not include this in the measurement.

2 **Cut the remaining lengths.** Thread a head pin through an end link of the cut chain, then through an end link of the original chain. Line up the chain links, and cut the next length of chain to match the first. Repeat to cut the remaining pieces needed.

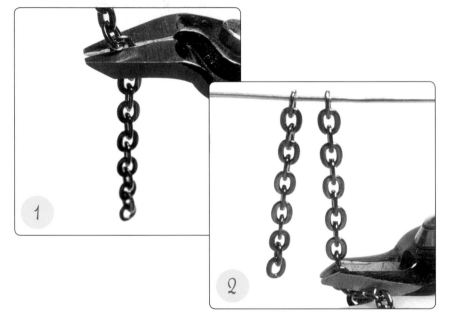

Open-Link Chain

Open chain links can be opened and closed just like jump rings (see page 14). Instead of cutting open-link chain, you can open and close the links to separate the necessary lengths of chain.

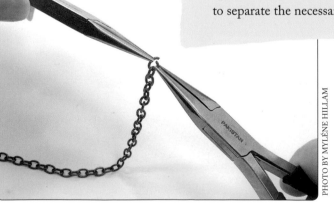

PHOTO BY MYLÈNE HILLAM

Forming a Loop

Round-nose pliers can be used to make loops in head pins, eye pins, or beading wire. Loops allow the pin or wire to be attached to other items using jump rings or other loops. Here's how to make a loop in an eye pin to create a bead link.

> Project(s) using this technique appear on pages 24, 28, 36, 40, 42, 46, 48, 50, 54, 56, 58, 60, and 62.

1 **Trim the pin.** Slide a bead (or beads) onto an eye pin. Using needle-nose pliers, bend the tail of the eye pin to form a right angle with the bead(s). Trim the tail about ¼" (0.5cm) beyond the last bead.

2 **Start forming the loop.** Grasp the end of the wire with round-nose pliers. Rotate your wrist to wrap the wire around the pliers, forming a loop. The jaws of the pliers taper, so the size of the loop can be adjusted based on its position in the pliers.

3 **Finish forming the loop.** You may need to release the pin, reposition the pliers, and rotate them again to completely close the loop.

4 **Check the finished link.** When finished, there will be a loop on each side of the bead so other components can be attached to each side.

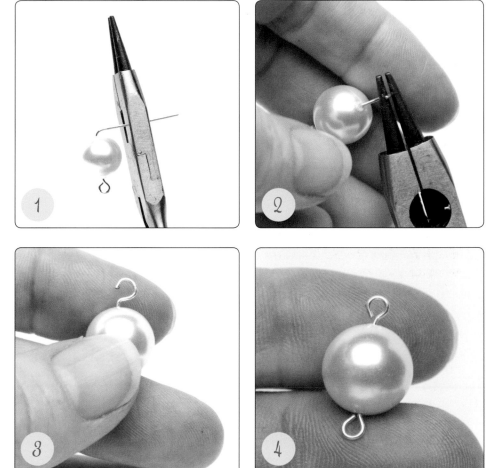

Tip: If you have trouble forming a loop at the end of a 1" (2.5cm) eye pin or head pin, you can always use a 2" (5cm) pin instead and simply trim off the excess.

Tip: You can convert a head pin to an eye pin by trimming off the flat head and forming a loop on that end instead.

Forming a Wrapped Loop

A wrapped loop is stronger than a basic loop, making it perfect for connecting heavy jewelry components. It also adds a decorative touch.

Project(s) using this technique appear on pages 46, 56, and 62.

1 *Bend the pin.* Slide a bead (or beads) onto a head pin. Grasp the head pin with round-nose pliers, resting the pliers against the top of the bead. Bend the tail of the pin to form a right angle with the bead(s).

2 *Start forming the loop.* Reposition the pliers so one prong is below the bend in the wire and one prong is above it. Wrap the tail of the head pin around the top prong, forming a loop.

3 *Finish forming the loop.* Reposition the pliers so the bottom prong is in the loop formed in Step 2. Finish forming the loop by wrapping the tail of the head pin around the bottom prong.

4 *Make the wrap.* Holding the loop with the pliers, wrap the tail of the head pin around the stem of the loop from the bottom of the loop to the top of the bead(s). Once the wrap is complete, trim away any excess from the tail of the head pin.

5 *Secure the tail.* Use needle-nose pliers or crimping pliers to tuck the trimmed tail into the wrap.

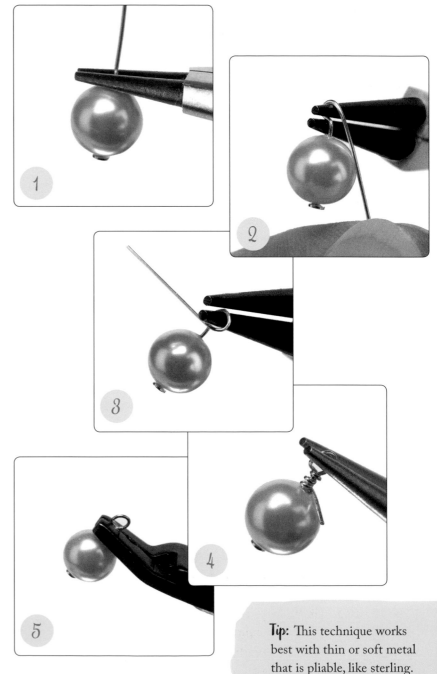

Tip: This technique works best with thin or soft metal that is pliable, like sterling.

Forming a Loop for Briolette Beads

Briolettes and other side-drilled beads require a slightly different technique for creating a loop at the top of the bead. Adding a loop gives these types of beads the appearance of a pendant or bead drop.

Project(s) using this technique appear on page 28.

1 *Make the stem.* Grasp an eye pin directly under the loop with round-nose pliers. Partially bend the tail of the pin to the side at about a 45-degree angle, below the prong of the pliers, to form a short stem under the loop.

2 *Position the pin.* With the bead flat on a surface, set the loop and stem directly above the top of the bead with the bent tail off to one side of the bead. Use the pliers to slightly mark the spot on the tail of the pin where the pin will need to bend to go into the bead hole.

3 *Make the first bend.* Thread the tail of the pin through the bead up to the spot marked in Step 2. Then bend the wire flush up against the bead to reposition the loop and stem at the top of the bead. Press the pin against the bead to shape it to the curve of the bead, using round-nose pliers to help shape it as needed.

4 *Make the second bend.* Bend the other end of the pin flush up against the other side of the bead to mirror your first bend, smoothing the pin against the side of the bead.

5 *Make the wrap.* Wrap the tail of the pin around the stem from the top of the bead to the bottom of the loop. Trim away any excess from the tail of the pin, and use needle-nose pliers or crimping pliers to tuck the tail into the wrap.

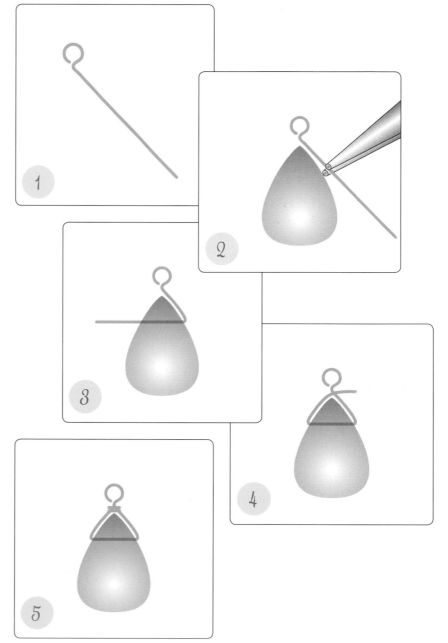

Overhand Knot

Overhand knots can be used to start or finish a design, to hold components in place in a design, or to function as decorative elements.

Project(s) using this technique appear on page 30.

Here is how to make a simple overhand knot.

To tie an overhand knot with a loop, fold the cord in half to form a loop at the center. Then tie the knot as usual, positioning the loop so it extends out of the knot.

Ready, Set, Craft!

The necklace shown here uses the techniques Opening and Closing Jump Rings as well as Cutting Chain. Go to page 44 to make this piece now, or just turn the page to get started with all of the stunning projects in this book!

Step-by-Step Projects

Now that you know the lingo and understand the basic techniques, it's
time to put what you've learned into practice and make some projects.
Remember to use the shopping lists to help navigate the jewelry section
at the store. And don't be afraid to choose materials that create a bold
statement and suit your personal taste to make a project your own!

Level:

Time:

The "Level" for each project indicates whether it is Beginner,
Intermediate, or Advanced.

The "Time" for each project indicates how long each project
will take, not including glue drying time. One diamond means
less than an hour; two diamonds means between one and two
hours; and three diamonds means more than two hours.

Level:
♦ ● ●

Time:
♦ ● ●

Deco Fringe Necklace

This design is a great everyday piece. The bold pendant makes a statement, while the simple chain keeps it from being over the top. Try this with a tailored work outfit to express your style in a professional setting.

1 *Make the bead links.* Slide a bicone, a rondelle spacer, and a bicone onto an eye pin and form a loop. Repeat to make a total of 6 bicone bead links. Slide a 6mm rhinestone round bead onto an eye pin and form a loop. Repeat to make a total of 8 rhinestone round bead links.

2 *Cut the chains.* Cut the following lengths of figure-8 chain: one 6" (15.5cm), eight 2" (5cm), and one 12" (31cm). Cut six 1½" (3.8cm) lengths of flat-link chain that have a round bead at one end of each length.

3 *Connect half of the necklace.* Connect the following to one end of the 6" (15.5cm) chain, in order: a bicone bead link, a 2" (5cm) figure-8 chain, a rhinestone round bead link, a 2" (5cm) chain, a bicone bead link, a 2" (5cm) chain, a rhinestone round bead link, a 2" (5cm) chain, and a bicone bead link.

4 *Finish the necklace.* Connect the 12" (31cm) chain to the last bead link from Step 3. Starting at the other end of the 12" (31cm) chain, repeat the connections from Step 3 in reverse order. When you are finished, thread the 6" (15.5cm) chain through the bail, then connect the 6" (15.5cm) chain to the last bicone bead link on the other end of the necklace.

5 *Start the pendant.* Use a 4mm jump ring to connect the top of the filigree connector to the bottom of the bail. Use 4mm jump rings to connect 2 lengths of flat-link chain from Step 2 to each of the two outer loops and to the middle loop at the bottom of the filigree connector.

6 *Finish the pendant.* Cut two 6-link and two 3-link lengths of chain from between the round beads of the flat-link chain. Use 4mm jump rings to connect the following, in order, to each of the two empty loops on the bottom of the filigree connector: a 6-link chain, a rhinestone round bead link from Step 1, a 3-link chain, and a rhinestone round bead link from Step 1.

SHOPPING LIST

- 12 - 6mm glass bicone beads (smoke)
- 8 - 6mm rhinestone round beads (black/crystal)
- 6 - 4 x 8mm rhinestone rondelle spacer beads (black/silver)
- 1 - Filigree connector (black/silver)
- 16" (41cm) - 1.5mm flat-link cable chain with 3mm round beads (gunmetal)
- 34" (87cm) - 5mm figure-8 chain (silver)
- 1 - Bail (gunmetal)
- 14 - 1" (2.5cm) eye pins (silver)
- 6 - 4mm jump rings (silver)

TOOLS

- Needle-nose pliers
- Round-nose pliers
- Wire cutters

TECHNIQUES

- Opening and Closing Jump Rings
- Cutting Chain
- Forming a Loop

Vintage Charm Necklace

This necklace is a twist on the classic charm bracelet. The antique gold chain and charms give it a vintage feel, but it can also be made with bright gold or silver chain with colorful charms. Be sure to include at least one word charm with a sentiment that's inspirational to you.

1   *Add the clasp.* Cut a 19" (49cm) length of chain. Use jump rings to connect each half of the toggle clasp to each end of the chain.

2   *Arrange the charms.* Place charms along the length of chain as desired. Try overlaying some charms or attaching charms to other charms.

3   *Attach the charms.* Use jump rings to connect the charms to the chain.

SHOPPING LIST

- 20–24 - Various vintage-inspired charms
- 19" (49cm) - 7mm double-link curb chain (antique gold)
- 22–26 - 6mm jump rings (antique gold)
- 1 - Toggle clasp set (copper)

TOOLS

- Needle-nose pliers
- Wire cutters

TECHNIQUES

- Opening and Closing Jump Rings
- Cutting Chain

Desert Blues Drop Necklace

Level: ◆ ● ●

Time: ◆ ● ●

The unique chain drops of this necklace create a lariat-style look. Shortened chain drops can be turned into matching earrings. Pair this design with oranges or corals, or change up the color of the beads for a totally different look.

1 *Make the bead drops.* Use an eye pin to form a loop on a turquoise spike drop. Repeat to make a total of 8 turquoise bead drops.

2 *Start the tassel.* Cut a 4½" (11.5cm), 4" (10cm), and 3½" (8.5cm) length of 4mm curb chain. Connect one end of all 3 chains to a 6mm jump ring.

3 *Finish the tassel.* Use a 4mm jump ring to attach a round charm to the other end of each of the lengths of chain from Step 2.

4 *Attach the tassel.* Cut a 30" (76cm) length of 8.5mm curb chain. Use an 8mm jump ring to join the two ends of the chain together. Connect the 6mm jump ring at the top of the tassel to the 8mm jump ring.

5 *Attach the bead drops.* Use a 6mm jump ring to attach 2 turquoise bead drops to the 8mm jump ring. Use 6mm jump rings to connect 3 turquoise bead drops, spaced 4 chain links apart, on each side of the 8mm jump ring.

SHOPPING LIST

- 3 - 10mm round charms (copper/teal)
- 8 - 28 x 5mm spike drops (turquoise)
- 30" (76cm) - 8.5mm curb chain (copper)
- 12" (31cm) - 4mm curb chain (copper)
- 8 - 2" (5cm) eye pins (copper)
- 3 - 4mm jump rings (copper)
- 8 - 6mm jump rings (copper)
- 1 - 8mm jump ring (copper)

TOOLS

- Needle-nose pliers
- Round-nose pliers
- Wire cutters

TECHNIQUES

- Opening and Closing Jump Rings
- Cutting Chain
- Forming a Loop
- Forming a Loop for Briolette Beads

Noir Rope Necklace

A swirling knot gives this necklace a nautical theme. Try it with navy rope for an even stronger nautical feel, or white or cream rope for a coastal vibe. This design will pair beautifully with your casual summer attire, or can be dressed up for a more formal night out.

1 **Prepare the rope.** Cut a 118" (300cm) length of rope. Fold the rope in half and form an overhand knot with a loop about 1" (2.5cm) below the fold.

2 **Add the first wire.** Cut a 1½" (4cm) length of flat wire. Using round-nose pliers, form each end of the wire into a separate channel. Thread each end of the rope through a channel.

3 **Prepare to knot.** Position the wire about 8" (20cm) below the overhand knot from Step 1 so the curved channels are on the underside. Tape the rope ends down just below the wire.

4 **Make the knot.** About 2" (5cm) past the wire, begin knotting the two ropes, following the illustration.

SHOPPING LIST

- 1 - 12mm round bead with 6mm hole (silver)
- 10' (305cm) - 3mm cotton rope cord (black)
- 3" (8cm) - 5mm aluminum flat wire (silver)

TOOLS

- Round-nose pliers
- Wire cutters
- Scissors
- Tape

TECHNIQUES

- Overhand Knot

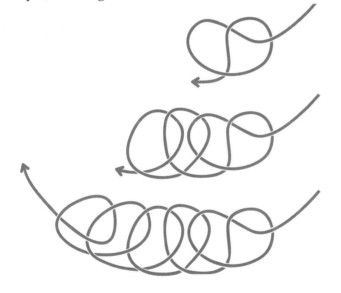

5 **Add the second wire.** Repeat Step 2 on the other side of the completed knot, about 2" (5cm) past the knot.

6 **Finish the necklace.** About 8" (20cm) beyond the second wire, form another overhand knot. Tape the rope ends together, forming the tape into a point. Thread both rope ends through the round bead. Remove the tape, fray the ends of the rope ends, and trim excess rope. If the bead is loose, add some glue.

Aztec Bib Necklace

Level:
◆◆●

Time:
♥♥●

The bold tribal look of this necklace is a perfect match for your summer wardrobe. Pair it with a strapless dress or a collared shirt, or use it to fill in a deep neckline. Keep the look natural with other jute cord accessories, or add more bling with additional gold and silver pieces.

1 **Cut the cords.** Cut the following lengths of 3mm silver-studded cord: 5" (12.7cm), 7" (17.8cm), 3¾" (9.5cm), 2½" (6.4cm), and 1" (2.5cm). Cut the following lengths of gold-studded brown cord (so that the studs match on both sides of the cuts): 6" (15.3cm) and 2" (5cm). Cut the following lengths of gold-studded tan cord (so that the studs match on both sides of the cuts): 8" (20.3cm) and 2" (5cm). Cut the following lengths of brown braided jute cord: 12" (30.5cm) and 8" (20.3cm). Cut 10 individual silver cones off the cone cord.

2 **Attach the cords.** Using the photo as a placement guide, glue the lengths of cord onto the bib base and allow to dry. For the tan, brown, and silver studded cords, trim the ends of the cords flush with the bib base, or fold the ends over and glue them to the back of the bib base. For the jute cord, tie the ends with thread to stabilize them, then wrap the ends around to the back of the bib base and glue them down.

3 **Glue the cones.** Glue 6 silver cones evenly spaced along the length of the top section of jute. Glue 4 silver cones evenly spaced along the length of the bottom section of jute. Allow to dry.

4 **Cut the chains.** Cut four 6½" (16.5cm) lengths of each of the 3 types of chain. Divide the chain lengths into 2 sets of 2 lengths of each type.

5 **Attach the chains.** Use an 8mm jump ring to connect the ends of one set of chains to the holes on one side of the top of the necklace base. Repeat with the other set of chains on the other side of the necklace base.

6 **Add the clasp.** Use 8mm jump rings to connect the ends of each set of chains together. Use a 6mm jump ring to connect one 8mm jump ring to one half of the toggle clasp. Repeat with the other set of chains and the other half of the toggle clasp.

> **Tip:** The measurements given in the Shopping List are approximate, depending on the size and shape of the bib base used. These instructions are for a bib base measuring 6" x 6" (15.3 x 15.3cm) at its widest dimensions. You may wish to substitute cord and create your own cording patterns.

SHOPPING LIST

- 1 - Acrylic bib necklace base (clear)
- 24" (61cm) - 3mm-wide silver-studded cord (silver)
- 12" (31cm) - 4mm-wide suede gold-studded cord (brown)
- 14" (36cm) - 4mm-wide suede gold-studded cord (tan)
- 8" (21cm) - 8mm-wide silver-studded cone cord (silver)
- 20" (51cm) - 14mm-wide natural braided jute cord (brown)
- 28" (72cm) - 1.8mm curb chain (gold)
- 28" (72cm) - 4mm flat-link cable chain (antique gold)
- 28" (72cm) - 4 x 7mm drawn cable chain (copper)
- 36" (92cm) - Sewing thread (tan)
- 4 - 8mm jump rings (gold)
- 2 - 6mm jump rings (gold)
- 1 - Nut and bolt toggle clasp set (gold)

TOOLS

- Needle-nose pliers
- Wire cutters
- Scissors
- E-6000® glue

TECHNIQUES

- Opening and Closing Jump Rings
- Cutting Chain

Level:
♦ ♦ ●

Time:
♦ ♦ ●

Turquoise Rose Necklace

This necklace is beautiful in its simplicity. Match the style in your wardrobe with sleek, simple pieces like a sheath dress or a blouse and cardigan. Extra materials can be used to make a matching bracelet. For a bolder statement, use brighter beads.

1 *Make the roses.* Use round-nose pliers to form a small, tight loop/fold at the beginning of the roll of silver twisted wire. Continue twisting the wire in a circular motion to form a dimensional rose about 1" (2.5cm) in diameter. Cut the wire off the roll, leaving enough wire to bring wire around to the back side of the rose and tuck it up in between the wrapped wires to hide the wire end. Repeat to make a total of 7 wire roses.

2 *Add the clasp.* Cut a 26" (66cm) length of beading wire. Use a crimp tube to connect one end of the beading wire to one half of the arrow toggle clasp. Trim excess wire.

3 *Start stringing.* String on the following: 10 turquoise rondelles, 1 silver rondelle spacer, 2 turquoise rondelles, 1 silver rondelle spacer, 3 turquoise rondelles, 1 silver rondelle spacer, 4 turquoise rondelles, and 1 silver rondelle spacer.

4 *Add the roses.* String on 1 turquoise rondelle. Then weave the beading wire through a wire rose. Repeat this pattern of 1 rondelle and 1 rose a total of 7 times, using up all of the wire roses.

5 *Finishing stringing.* String on 1 turquoise rondelle. Then continue stringing by repeating Step 3 in reverse.

6 *Finish the clasp.* Use a crimp tube to connect the end of the beading wire to the other half of the arrow toggle clasp. Trim excess wire.

SHOPPING LIST

- 46 - 8mm rondelle beads (turquoise)
- 8 - 4 x 8mm rhinestone rondelle spacer beads (silver)
- 26" (66cm) - Beading wire (silver)
- 72" (185cm) - 5mm aluminum twisted wire (silver)
- 2 - Crimp tubes (silver)
- 1 - Arrow toggle clasp set (silver)

TOOLS

- Round-nose pliers
- Crimping pliers
- Wire cutters

TECHNIQUES

- Attaching Crimp Tubes/Beads

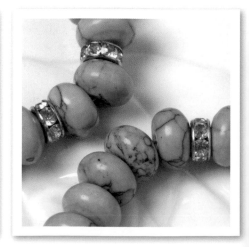

Rainbow Crystal Necklace

With its bright, bold design, this necklace provides loads of fun, funky flair. Allow this piece to shine by keeping other accessories and your outfit simple. A neutral top will let the colors pop.

1 *Cut the wire.* Cut the following lengths of beading wire: one 20" (51cm), two 22" (56cm), and one 25" (64cm).

2 *Make the pink strand.* Use a crimp tube to connect one end of a 22" (56cm) beading wire to a lobster clasp. String on 1 peach round and 1 pink puffed square. Repeat this 2-bead pattern 4 more times. Next, string on 1 peach round, 1 pink rectangle, 1 peach round, and 1 pink oblong. Repeat this 4-bead pattern 3 more times. Next, string on 1 peach round, 1 pink rectangle, and 1 peach round. Next, string on 1 pink puffed square and 1 peach round. Repeat this 2-bead pattern 4 more times. Use a crimp tube to connect the end of this bead strand to a 6mm jump ring. Attach the extender chain to the jump ring.

3 *Make the yellow strand.* Use a crimp tube to connect one end of a 22" (56cm) beading wire to a 4mm jump ring. Connect the jump ring to the pink strand of beading wire between the fourth pink puffed square and the fifth peach round on one side of the strand. String the following onto the 22" (56cm) wire: 4 yellow rondelles, 1 yellow puffed octagon, 1 pink pearl, 1 yellow puffed octagon, and 1 pink pearl. Next, string on 1 yellow oblong, 1 pink pearl, 1 yellow puffed octagon, and 1 pink pearl. Repeat this 4-bead pattern 3 more times. String on 1 yellow puffed octagon and 4 yellow rondelles. Use a crimp tube to connect the end of this strand to a 4mm jump ring. Connect that jump ring to the other side of the pink strand between the fourth pink puffed square and the fifth peach round.

4 *Make the green strand.* Use a crimp tube to connect one end of the 20" (51cm) beading wire to a 4mm jump ring. Connect the jump ring to the yellow strand of beading wire between the second yellow puffed octagon and the second pink pearl on one side of the strand. String the following onto the 20" (51cm) wire: 3 yellow rondelles. Next, string on 1 green cube and 1 yellow rondelle. Repeat this 2-bead pattern 2 more times. Next, string on 1 green trapezoid and 1 green cube. Repeat this 2-bead pattern 2 more times. String on 1 green trapezoid. Next, string on 1 yellow rondelle and 1 green cube. Repeat this 2-bead pattern 2 more times. String on 3 yellow rondelles. Use a crimp tube to connect the end of this bead strand to a 4mm

SHOPPING LIST

- 26 - 6mm acrylic faceted round beads (peach)
- 10 - 10mm acrylic faceted puffed square beads (light pink)
- 5 - 23 x 20mm acrylic faceted flat rectangle beads (light pink)
- 4 - 28 x 20mm acrylic swirl flat oblong beads (light pink)
- 20 - 6mm acrylic faceted rondelle beads (yellow)
- 7 - 16mm acrylic faceted puffed octagon beads (yellow)
- 10 - 7mm acrylic round beads (light pink pearl)
- 4 - 28 x 20mm acrylic swirl flat oblong beads (yellow)
- 9 - 8mm acrylic cube beads (green)
- 4 - 30 x 24mm acrylic swirl flat trapezoid beads (light green)
- 20 - 6mm acrylic faceted rondelle beads (aqua)
- 9 - 13 x 11mm acrylic oval beads (aqua pearl)
- 6 - 16mm acrylic faceted puffed octagon beads (aqua)
- 4 - 30 x 24mm acrylic swirl flat trapezoid beads (aqua)
- 10 - 16 x 12mm acrylic flat diamond beads (cobalt blue)
- 8' (245cm) - Beading wire (silver)
- 8 - Crimp tubes (silver)
- 1 - 3" (7.5cm) extender chain (silver)
- 10 - 1" (2.5cm) head pins (silver)
- 6 - 4mm jump rings (silver)
- 1 - 6mm jump ring (silver)
- 1 - Lobster clasp (silver)

TOOLS

- Needle-nose pliers
- Round-nose pliers
- Crimping pliers
- Wire cutters

TECHNIQUES

- Opening and Closing Jump Rings
- Attaching Crimp Tubes/Beads
- Forming a Loop

jump ring. Connect that jump ring to the other side of the yellow strand between the second yellow puffed octagon and the second pink pearl.

5 *Make the bead drops.* Slide a blue diamond onto a head pin and form a loop. Repeat to make a total of 10 bead drops.

6 *Make the blue strand.* Use a crimp tube to connect one end of the 25" (64cm) beading wire to a 4mm jump ring. Connect this jump ring to the 4mm jump ring connecting the yellow strand to the pink strand on one side of the necklace. String the following onto the 25" (64cm) wire: 3 peach rounds, 6 aqua rondelles, and 1 aqua puffed octagon. Next, string on 1 aqua pearl oval and 1 aqua puffed octagon. Repeat this 2-bead pattern 1 more time. String on 1 bead drop, 1 aqua pearl oval, and 1 bead drop. Next, string on 1 aqua rondelle, 1 aqua trapezoid, 1 aqua rondelle, 1 bead drop, 1 aqua pearl oval, and 1 bead drop. Repeat this 6-bead pattern 3 more times. Next, string on 1 aqua puffed octagon and 1 aqua pearl oval. Repeat this 2-bead pattern 1 more time. String on 1 aqua puffed octagon, 6 aqua rondelles, and 3 peach rounds. Use a crimp tube to connect the end of this bead strand to a 4mm jump ring. Connect that jump ring to the 4mm jump ring connecting the yellow strand to the pink strand on the other side of the necklace.

Violet Medallion Necklace

Level: ◆◆◇
Time: ◆◆◇

The components in this design give a nod to Spanish style. Try it with a messy side bun or an updo. This piece will stand out against creams, yellows, and greens. Or you can give it a subtler look by pairing it with a black top.

1 **Cut the wire.** Cut one 9" (23cm), one 15" (38cm), and three 12" (31cm) lengths of beading wire.

2 **String one side of the necklace.** Connect a jump ring to the outer edge of a pendant directly across from the loop on the pendant. Use a crimp tube to connect one end of a 12" (31cm) length of wire to the jump ring. String on 1 purple bicone and 1 rondelle. Repeat until you have strung on a total of 20 of each type of bead. Use another crimp tube to connect the other end of the wire to a jump ring. Trim excess wire.

3 **String the other side of the necklace.** Repeat Step 2 to make another identical beaded wire on the other pendant. Connect the lobster clasp to the jump ring at the end of this second wire.

4 **String the short middle strand.** Use a crimp tube to connect one end of the 9" (23cm) beading wire to the loop on one of the pendants. String on 1 rondelle and 1 purple oval. Then, string on 1 clear bicone and 1 purple oval. Repeat this 2-bead pattern until you have strung on a total of 6 purple ovals and 5 clear bicones. End the strand with 1 more rondelle. Use a crimp tube to connect the other end of the wire to the loop on the other pendant.

5 **String the medium middle strand.** Use a crimp tube to connect one end of a 12" (31cm) beading wire to the loop on one of the pendants so that the new wire hangs underneath the beaded 9" (23cm) wire. String on 1 rondelle and 1 purple oval. Then, string on 1 clear bicone and 1 purple oval. Repeat this 2-bead pattern until you have strung on a total of 9 purple ovals and 8 clear bicones. End the strand with 1 more rondelle. Use a crimp tube to connect the other end of the wire to the loop on the other pendant so that this strand hangs underneath the beaded 9" (23cm) strand. Trim excess wire.

6 **String the long middle strand.** Bring one end of the 15" (38cm) length of beading wire through one pendant about ½" (1.5cm) to the outside of the loop on that pendant. Use a crimp tube to connect the end of this wire to the pendant. String on 1 rondelle and 1 purple oval. Then, string on 1 clear bicone and 1 purple oval. Repeat this 2-bead pattern until you have strung on a total of 12 purple ovals and 11 clear bicones. End the strand with 1 more rondelle. Use a crimp tube to connect the other end of the wire to the corresponding spot in the other pendant so that this strand hangs underneath the beaded 12" (31cm) strand. Trim excess wire.

SHOPPING LIST

- 2 - 36.5mm pendants with open design (purple/silver)
- 40 - 4mm glass bicone beads (light purple)
- 24 - 4mm glass bicone beads (clear)
- 46 - 10mm rondelle beads (mirror purple/blue)
- 27 - 13 x 10mm acrylic ovals (matte purple)
- 60" (155cm) - Beading wire (silver)
- 10 - Crimp tubes (silver)
- 4 - 6mm jump rings (silver)
- 1 - Lobster clasp (silver)

TOOLS

- Needle-nose pliers
- Round-nose pliers
- Crimping pliers
- Wire cutters

TECHNIQUES

- Opening and Closing Jump Rings
- Attaching Crimp Tubes/Beads

Chandelier Necklace

In elegant neutrals, this necklace has a classic, chic look made for a night out. Match the style with a sleek black dress and a simple updo. Make two extra bead drops in Step 3 and attach them to earring wires to make a matching pair of earrings.

1 *Make the chains.* Cut twelve 8" (21cm) lengths of chain. Divide the chains into 2 sets of 6. Use 6mm jump rings to connect the end links together on both ends of each separate set of chains. Use a 4mm jump ring to connect a lobster clasp to one 6mm jump ring on one set of chains. Attach another 6mm jump ring to one 6mm jump ring on the other set of chains. This end will be the clasp end.

2 *Add 2 connectors.* Use 4mm jump rings to attach the top of a faceted connector to each of the single 6mm jump rings on both sets of chain.

3 *Make the large bead drops.* Slide a white round onto an eye pin and form a loop to make a bead link. Slide a 4mm black bicone onto a head pin and form a loop to make a small bead drop. Connect the small bead drop to one end of the bead link to make a large bead drop. Repeat to make a total of 4 large bead drops.

4 *Add the bead drops.* Connect a large bead drop to the outside edge of the 6mm jump ring at the bottom of each set of chain, where the faceted connector is connected. Connect a large bead drop to the outside edge loop on the bottom of each faceted connector.

5 *Connect the faceted connectors.* Connect a 4mm jump ring to the loop on the inside edge of the bottom of each faceted connector. Use another 4mm jump ring to connect those 2 jump rings, connecting the connectors.

6 *Make the small bead drops.* Slide a 6mm black bicone onto a head pin and form a loop to make a small bead drop. Repeat to make a total of 2 small bead drops. Connect a small bead drop to the bottom middle loop on each faceted pendant.

7 *Finish the necklace.* Slide a white round onto an eye pin and form a loop to make a bead link. Connect the bead link to the bottom of the middle 4mm jump ring from Step 5. Use another 4mm jump ring to connect the other side of the bead link to the bail on the oval pendant.

SHOPPING LIST

- 1 - 50 x 30mm oval gem pendant with bail (silver/black)
- 2 - 52 x 26mm faceted gem connectors (black/white)
- 5 - 6mm round beads (white)
- 4 - 4mm glass bicone beads (black)
- 2 - 6mm glass bicone beads (black)
- 8' (255cm) - 2.5 x 2mm curb chain (silver)
- 6 - 1" (2.5cm) head pins (silver)
- 5 - 1" (2.5cm) eye pins (silver)
- 7 - 4mm jump rings (silver)
- 5 - 6mm jump rings (silver)
- 1 - Lobster clasp (silver)

TOOLS

- Needle-nose pliers
- Round-nose pliers
- Wire cutters

TECHNIQUES

- Opening and Closing Jump Rings
- Cutting Chain
- Forming a Loop

Edgy Angles Gem Necklace

The bead drop and angles at the front of this necklace create a unique, eye-catching look. This piece can be used to dress up a simple t-shirt or paired with more formal work attire. Additional gold accents will highlight the gold undertones in this design.

1 *Cut the chain and wire.* Cut the following lengths of chain: 2" (5cm), 2¼" (5.7cm), and 3" (7.6cm). Cut two 8" (20.5cm) lengths of beading wire.

2 *Make the bead links and drop.* Slide a twist bead onto a head pin and form a loop to make a twist bead drop. Slide a twist bead onto an eye pin and form a loop to make a twist bead link. Repeat to make a total of 4 twist bead links. Slide a trapezoid onto an eye pin and form a loop to make a trapezoid bead link. Repeat to make a total of 3 trapezoid bead links. Slide a brown flat rectangle onto an eye pin and form a loop to make a rectangle bead link.

3 *Start the necklace.* Connect the following, in order: 1 twist bead drop, 1 twist bead link, and 1 trapezoid bead link. Use a 4mm jump ring to connect the other side of the trapezoid bead link to one end of the 2" (5cm) chain and 1 twist bead link. Use a 4mm jump ring to connect the other side of the twist bead link to a trapezoid bead link and one end of the 2¼" (5.7cm) chain. Use a 4mm jump ring to connect the other side of the trapezoid bead link to a twist bead link and one end of the 3" (7.6cm) chain. Connect the other side of the twist bead link to a rectangle bead link.

4 *String one side.* Use a crimp bead to connect the end of one length of beading wire from Step 1 to the other end of the rectangle bead link from Step 3. String the following onto the wire: 1 clear puffed square, 1 twist bead, 1 brown cube, 1 metallic brown octagon rectangle, 1 brown cube, 1 orange/ecru flat oval, 1 clear puffed square, 1 brown puffed square, 1 clear cube, 1 metallic brown octagon rectangle, 1 brown puffed square, and 1 bronze dimpled round. Use a crimp bead to connect the end of the beading wire to one half of the toggle clasp.

5 *Start the other side.* Use a 6mm jump to connect the loose ends of the 2" (5cm), 2¼" (5.7cm), and 3" (7.6cm) chains together so they hang from shortest to longest. Use a 4mm jump ring to connect the 6mm jump ring to a twist bead link. Connect the other end of the bead link to a trapezoid bead link.

SHOPPING LIST

- 3 - 30 x 24mm acrylic swirl trapezoid beads (brown)
- 2 - 23 x 20mm acrylic faceted flat rectangle beads (brown)
- 10 - 10mm faceted glass twist beads (mirror gold/clear)
- 1 - 18 x 13mm faceted flat oval bead (orange/ecru)
- 1 - 12mm acrylic cube bead (clear)
- 3 - 12mm acrylic cube beads (brown)
- 2 - 5mm dimpled round beads (bronze)
- 3 - 9mm acrylic puffed square beads (brown)
- 4 - 9mm acrylic puffed square beads (clear)
- 3 - 15 x 10mm acrylic octagon rectangle beads (metallic brown)
- 1 - 20 x 12mm acrylic tri-oval bead (copper)
- 8" (21cm) - 4mm curb chain (gold)
- 16" (41cm) - Beading wire (gold)
- 4 - Crimp beads (gold)
- 8 - 2" (5cm) eye pins (gold)
- 1 - 1" (2.5cm) head pin (gold)
- 4 - 4mm jump rings (gold)
- 1 - 6mm jump ring (gold)
- 1 - Toggle clasp set (gold)

TOOLS

- Needle-nose pliers
- Round-nose pliers
- Crimping pliers
- Wire cutters

TECHNIQUES

- Opening and Closing Jump Rings
- Attaching Crimp Tubes/Beads
- Cutting Chain
- Forming a Loop

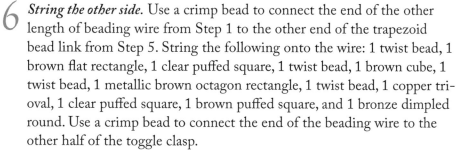

6 *String the other side.* Use a crimp bead to connect the end of the other length of beading wire from Step 1 to the other end of the trapezoid bead link from Step 5. String the following onto the wire: 1 twist bead, 1 brown flat rectangle, 1 clear puffed square, 1 twist bead, 1 brown cube, 1 twist bead, 1 metallic brown octagon rectangle, 1 twist bead, 1 copper tri-oval, 1 clear puffed square, 1 brown puffed square, and 1 bronze dimpled round. Use a crimp bead to connect the end of the beading wire to the other half of the toggle clasp.

Ombré Fringe Necklace

Level: ◈ ◈ ●

Time: ◈ ◈ ●

The chain fringe of this necklace keeps it light and airy with lots of movement while still making a bold statement. The single top chain adds a special touch to the overall design. Pair this with a light-colored outfit to let the ombré pattern stand out.

1 **Cut the main chains.** Cut a 17" (43cm) and an 18" (46cm) length of gold chain. Use 4mm gold jump rings to attach the ends of each chain to each half of the toggle clasp so that the 18" (46cm) chain drapes below the 17" (43cm) chain.

2 **Cut the gold fringe.** Cut twenty-seven 2" (5cm) lengths of gold chain.

3 **Attach the gold fringe.** Use a 4mm gold jump ring to connect one of the 2" (5cm) gold chains to the bottom center of the 18" (46cm) gold chain. Use 4mm gold jump rings to connect one end of thirteen 2" (5cm) chains onto the 18" (46cm) length chain on each side of the center 2" (5cm) chain, skipping a link between each chain.

4 **Attach the antique gold fringe.** Cut twenty-seven 2" (5cm) lengths of antique gold chain. Use 4mm antique gold jump rings to connect one end of each of these chains to the bottom of each of the 2" (5cm) gold chains.

5 **Attach the black fringe.** Cut twenty-seven 2" (5cm) lengths of black chain. Use 4mm black jump rings to connect one end of each of these chains to the bottom of each of the 2" (5cm) antique gold chains.

SHOPPING LIST

- 9' (275cm) - 4mm cable chain (gold)
- 64" (165cm) - 3mm flat-link cable chain (antique gold)
- 64" (165cm) - 5mm cable chain (black)
- 31 - 4mm jump rings (gold)
- 27 - 4mm jump rings (antique gold)
- 27 - 4mm jump rings (black)
- 1 - 33 x 29mm deco toggle clasp set (gold/black)

TOOLS

- Needle-nose pliers (2 pairs)
- Wire cutters

TECHNIQUES

- Opening and Closing Jump Rings
- Cutting Chain

Chunky Stone Necklace

This necklace has it all—bold colors, natural elements, and a fun tassel. Use it to add unique flair to a work outfit or cocktail dress. The orange pendant will stand out against blue or turquoise colors. For a different look, use silver chain and a blue or turquoise pendant.

1 *Cut the chain.* Cut the following lengths of chain: six ⅝" (1.6cm), four 2½" (6.5cm), one 5" (12.5cm), and two 12" (30.5cm).

2 *Make the tassel.* Use a 6mm jump ring to connect one end of each of the four 2½" (6.5cm) chains together. Then use another 6mm jump ring to connect the gathered chains to the bottom of a flower connector. Attach another 6mm jump ring to the top of the flower connector.

3 *Finish the pendant.* Thread an eye pin through the hole in the orange pendant and form a wrapped loop above the pendant. Attach a 6mm jump ring to the top of the wrapped loop. Use another 6mm jump ring to attach the 6mm jump ring at the top of the tassel from Step 2 to the pendant so it hangs down in front of the pendant.

4 *Make the bead links.* Thread an eye pin through the hole of an agate slice and form a loop to make an agate bead link. Repeat to make a total of 4 agate bead links.

5 *Connect one side of the necklace.* Connect the following, in order, to the 6mm jump ring at the top of the pendant from Step 3: a 6mm jump ring, a ⅝" (1.6cm) length of chain, an agate bead link, a ⅝" (1.6cm) length of chain, an agate bead link, a ⅝" (1.6cm) length of chain, a 6mm jump ring, a flower connector, a 6mm jump ring, and the middle link of a 12" (30.5cm) length of chain.

6 *Connect the other side of the necklace.* Repeat Step 5 to connect the other side of the necklace.

7 *Add the final chain.* Connect the ends of the 5" (12.5cm) chain to the bottom 6mm jump rings of the flower connectors on each side of the necklace.

8 *Add the clasp.* Use a 4mm jump ring to connect both ends of one 12" (30.5cm) chain to a lobster clasp. Connect another 4mm jump ring to both ends of the other 12" (30.5cm) chain.

SHOPPING LIST

- 1 - Resin pendant (orange)
- 4 - Various sizes of agate side-drilled slices (orange/tan)
- 3 - Flower connectors (copper/teal)
- 45" (115cm) - 4 x 8mm drawn cable chain (copper)
- 5 - 1" (2.5cm) eye pins (copper)
- 11 - 6mm jump rings (copper)
- 2 - 4mm jump rings (copper)
- 1 - Lobster clasp (copper)

TOOLS

- Needle-nose pliers
- Round-nose pliers
- Wire cutters

TECHNIQUES

- Opening and Closing Jump Rings
- Cutting Chain
- Forming a Loop
- Forming a Wrapped Loop

Black Pearl Treasure Necklace

This design is a twist on the classic pearl necklace—the unique shape and black color give it a modern look. Pair it with simple, elegant pieces from your closet, like a sheath dress. This design will also look great in other colors of pearl. Try gray, white, or cream.

1 *Make the 10 bead drops.* Slide a 14mm pearl onto a head pin and form a loop. Repeat to make a total of four 14mm single bead drops. Slide two 14mm pearls onto a head pin and form a loop to make one 14mm double bead drop. Slide a 14mm pearl and a 10mm pearl onto a head pin and form a loop. Repeat to make a total of two 10/14mm double bead drops. Slide a 10mm pearl onto head pin and form a loop. Repeat to make a total of three 10mm single bead drops.

2 *Make the 12 bead links.* Slide two 8mm pearls onto an eye pin and form a loop. Repeat to make a total of two 8mm double bead links. Slide a 6mm pearl, an 8mm pearl, and a 6mm pearl onto an eye pin and form a loop. Repeat to make a total of seven 6/8/6mm triple bead links. Slide a 14mm pearl onto an eye pin and form a loop. Repeat to make a total of three 14mm single bead links.

3 *Make the bead link/drop strands.* Connect the following, in order: an 8mm double bead link, 6mm jump ring, and a 10mm single bead drop. Repeat to make a total of two 8/10mm bead link/drop strands. Connect the following, in order: a 6/8/6mm triple bead link, a 6mm jump ring, and a single 14mm bead drop. Repeat to make a total of two 6/8/6/14mm bead link/drop strands. Connect the following, in order: a 6/8/6mm triple bead link, a 6mm jump ring, and a 10/14mm double bead drop. Repeat to make a total of two 6/8/6/10/14mm bead link/drop strands. Connect the following, in order: a 6/8/6mm triple bead link, a 6mm jump ring, a 14mm single bead link, and a 14mm single bead drop. Repeat to make a total of two 6/8/6/14/14mm bead link/drop strands.

4 *Start the necklace.* Cut a 22" (56cm) and a 26" (66cm) length of beading wire. Use crimp tubes to connect one end of each length of wire to a single 6mm jump ring. Connect the jump ring to one end of the extender chain. Connect a 10mm single bead drop to the other end of the extender chain.

5 *String one half of the top of the necklace.* String the following onto the 22" (56cm) length of wire: seventeen 6mm pearls, twelve 8mm pearls, the top loop of an 8/10mm bead link/drop strand, an 8mm pearl, the top loop of a 6/8/6/14mm bead link/drop strand, an 8mm pearl, the top loop of a 6/8/6/10/14mm bead link/drop strand, a 6mm pearl, the top loop of a 6/8/6/14/14mm bead link/drop strand, and a 6mm pearl.

SHOPPING LIST

- 96 - 6mm round beads (black pearl)
- 47 - 8mm round beads (black pearl)
- 23 - 10mm round beads (black pearl)
- 11 - 14mm round beads (black pearl)
- 48" (125cm) - Beading wire (silver)
- 4 - Crimp tubes (silver)
- 1 - 2" (5cm) extender chain (silver)
- 10 - 2" (5cm) head pins (silver)
- 12 - 2" (5cm) eye pins (silver)
- 10 - 6mm jump rings (silver)
- 1 - Lobster clasp (silver)

TOOLS

- Needle-nose pliers
- Round-nose pliers
- Crimping pliers
- Wire cutters

TECHNIQUES

- Opening and Closing Jump Rings
- Attaching Crimp Tubes/Beads
- Forming a Loop

6 *String the other half of the top of the necklace.* Connect the following, in order: a 6/8/6mm triple bead link, a 6mm jump ring, a 14mm single bead link, and the 14mm double bead link drop. String the top loop of this bead link/drop strand onto the 22" (56cm) beading wire. Then repeat Step 5 in reverse. Use a crimp tube to connect the other end of this beading wire to the loop on the lobster clasp.

7 *String one half of the bottom of the necklace.* String the following onto the 26" (66cm) length of wire: twenty-two 6mm pearls, four 8mm pearls, five 10mm pearls, the 6mm jump ring of an 8/10mm bead link/drop strand, a 10mm pearl, the 6mm jump ring of a 6/8/6/14mm bead link/drop strand, a 10mm pearl, the 6mm jump ring of a 6/8/6/10/14mm bead link/drop strand, a 10mm pearl, the 6mm jump ring of a 6/8/6/14/14mm bead link/drop strand, and a 10mm pearl.

8 *String the rest of the necklace.* String on the 6mm jump ring of the middle bead link/drop strand from Step 6, then repeat Step 7 in reverse. Use a crimp tube to connect the other end of this beading wire to the loop of the lobster clasp so that this strand hangs below the shorter strand.

Out on the Town Necklace

The chic black and white pendant gives this design an elegant touch, while the bead drops add lots of movement and sparkle. The combined effect makes this the perfect piece for a fun night out. Make two extra bead drops and attach them to earring wires for a matching pair of earrings.

1 *Make a bead link.* Slide a glitter bead, a rondelle, and a 6mm silver bead onto an eye pin and form a loop to create a bead link.

2 *Create the pendant.* Use a 4mm jump ring to connect the bottom loop of the bead link from Step 1 to the top loop of the chandelier pendant.

3 *Attach the pendant.* Cut a 22" (56cm) length of chain. Find the middle link of the chain and use a 4mm jump ring to connect the top loop of the bead link from Step 1 to this middle link.

4 *Make the small bead drops.* Slide a rondelle, a 6mm silver bead, and a 4mm silver bead onto a head pin and form a loop. Repeat to make a total of 10 small bead drops.

5 *Make the large bead drops.* Slide a glitter bead, a rondelle, and a 6mm silver bead onto a head pin and form a loop. Repeat to make a total of 8 large bead drops.

6 *Attach the small bead drops.* Use 4mm jump rings to attach small bead drops from Step 4 to the outside edge of the second link of chain up from the middle link, the sixth link up from the middle link, the tenth link up from the middle link, the fourteenth link up from the middle link, and the eighteenth link up from the middle link. Do this on both sides of the necklace.

7 *Attach the large bead drops.* Use 4mm jump rings to attach large bead drops from Step 5 to the outside edge of the fourth link of chain up from the middle link, the eighth link up from the middle link, the twelfth link up from the middle link, and the sixteenth link up from the middle link. Do this on both sides of the necklace.

8 *Attach the clasp.* Use a 4mm jump ring to attach a lobster clasp to one end of the necklace. Connect a 6mm jump ring to the other end of the necklace.

SHOPPING LIST

- 1 - 52 x 26mm faceted chandelier pendant (black & white)
- 9 - 10mm round beads (black/silver glitter)
- 19 - 8mm faceted rondelle beads (black/silver)
- 10 - 4mm round beads (mirror silver)
- 19 - 6mm round beads (mirror silver)
- 22" (56cm) - 8mm curb chain (silver)
- 18 - 2" (5cm) head pins (silver)
- 1 - 2" (5cm) eye pin (silver)
- 21 - 4mm jump rings (silver)
- 1 - 6mm jump ring (silver)
- 1 - Lobster clasp (silver)

TOOLS

- Needle-nose pliers
- Round-nose pliers
- Wire cutters

TECHNIQUES

- Opening and Closing Jump Rings
- Cutting Chain
- Forming a Loop

Golden Fan Necklace

This edgy design will pair with any color in your wardrobe. Try it with bright neons or chic neutrals. When wearing a bold statement necklace, remember to keep your earrings and other jewelry pieces simple.

1 *Prepare the chain.* Cut four 5½" (14cm) lengths of chain and divide them into pairs. Use a 4mm jump ring to join one end of a pair of chains to a lobster clasp. Use two 4mm jump rings, together, to join one end of the other pair of chains to the extender chain. (Two jump rings are used for added strength.)

2 *Prepare the wire.* Cut a 10" (26cm) and a 12" (31cm) length of beading wire. Use crimp tubes to connect one end of each wire to the loose end of a pair of chains so the longer wire sits below the shorter wire.

3 *String the top section.* String the following onto the 10" (26cm) wire: 1 gold round and the top hole of 1 slider bar. Repeat 11 more times and string on 1 more gold round after the last slider bar.

4 *Finish the top section.* Use a crimp tube to connect the other end of the top wire to the end of the top chain on the other side of the necklace. Trim excess wire.

5 *String the bottom section.* String the following onto the 12" (31cm) wire: 1 gold round, 1 spoon charm, and the bottom hole of the first slider bar from the top section. Then string on 3 spoons and the bottom hole of the next slider bar. Repeat stringing on 3 spoons and the bottom hole of the next slider bar 10 more times until all of the slider bars from the top section are attached to the 12" (31cm) wire. After the last slider bar, string on 1 spoon and 1 gold round.

6 *Finish the bottom section.* Use a crimp tube to connect the other end of the bottom wire to the end of the bottom chain on the other side of the necklace. Trim excess wire.

SHOPPING LIST

- 35 - 37 x 8.5mm spoon charms (gold)
- 12 - 10 x 6mm rhinestone slider bars (gunmetal)
- 15 - 8mm scroll round beads (gold)
- 24" (61cm) - 6mm rope chain (gunmetal)
- 22" (57cm) - Beading wire (silver)
- 4 - Crimp tubes (gunmetal)
- 1 - 2" (5cm) extender chain (gunmetal)
- 3 - 4mm jump rings (gunmetal)
- 1 - Lobster clasp (gunmetal)

TOOLS

- Needle-nose pliers
- Crimping pliers
- Wire cutters

TECHNIQUES

- Opening and Closing Jump Rings
- Attaching Crimp Tubes/Beads
- Cutting Chain

Spiked Scarf Necklace

This unique design uses chain to create a wrapped scarf look. The long dangles are a great way to jazz up a basic dress, or you can pair it with a plain t-shirt, jeans, cardigan, and boots for a more casual look.

1 *Make the main chains.* Using two pairs of pliers, separate the following lengths of large chain: 23½" (61cm), 25" (64cm), and 26" (67cm).

2 *Prepare the spacers.* Thread a head pin through each of the 2 outer edge holes of a 3-hole spacer and form loops. Thread an eye pin through the center hole of the spacer and form a loop. Repeat with the other spacer.

3 *Connect the chains.* Attach the 23½" (61cm) chain to the outer edge loop on one spacer, the 25" (64cm) chain to the center loop on the same side of the spacer, and the 26" (67cm) chain to the other outer edge loop. Connect the other ends of these chains to the corresponding loops of the other spacer.

4 *Add the clasp.* Using 6mm jump rings, attach a lobster clasp to the single outside center loop on one spacer, and attach an extender chain to the single outside center loop on the other spacer.

5 *Make the decorative chains.* Using two pairs of pliers, separate the following lengths of large chain: 13½" (34.5cm) and 14" (35.5cm). Cut 2 each of the following lengths of small chain: 11" (28cm), 12" (30.5cm), and 13" (33cm).

6 *Attach the decorative chains.* Use an 8mm jump ring to join together one end of 3 of the small chains (one of each length) and one end of 1 of the large chains from Step 5. Attach the 8mm jump ring to the last link of the 26" (67cm) chain next to one of the spacers. Repeat to attach the remaining chains to the other spacer.

7 *Add the spikes.* Use 6mm jump rings to attach a spike to the end of each of the decorative chains.

SHOPPING LIST

- 8 - 34mm spike charms (gold)
- 9' (275cm) - 9mm curb chain (antique gold)
- 72" (185cm) - 4mm flat-link cable chain (antique gold)
- 1 - 3" (7.5cm) extender chain (antique gold)
- 4 - 1" (2.5cm) head pins (antique gold)
- 2 - 1" (2.5cm) eye pins (antique gold)
- 10 - 6mm jump rings (antique gold)
- 2 - 8mm jump rings (antique gold)
- 2 - 26 x 9mm metal 3-hole spacers (gold)
- 1 - Lobster clasp (antique gold)

TOOLS

- Needle-nose pliers (2 pairs)
- Round-nose pliers
- Wire cutters

TECHNIQUES

- Opening and Closing Jump Rings
- Cutting Chain
- Forming a Loop

Rose Drop Necklace

The rose and antique gold colors of this necklace are beautifully set off by linen or other beige and cream fabrics. Enhance the vintage flair of the design with a top featuring peasant or bishop sleeves and additional antique gold jewelry pieces.

1 **Cut the chain.** Cut two 6½" (16.5cm) lengths of chain. Attach a 4mm jump ring to one end of each length of chain.

2 **Bead the bottom strand.** Cut a 12" (31cm) length of beading wire. Use a crimp tube to connect the wire to a jump ring on one of the chains from Step 1. String the following pattern onto the wire: 1 pearl, 1 wavy disc, 1 dagger, and 1 wavy disc. Repeat 14 more times and end with 1 more pearl. Use another crimp tube to connect the end of this bead strand to the 4mm jump ring on the end of the other 6½" (16.5cm) chain.

3 **Start the clasp.** Use a 4mm jump ring to attach a lobster clasp to the end of one of the lengths of chain from Step 1.

4 **Add the extender chain.** Connect one end of the extender chain to a 6mm jump ring. Connect the jump ring to the end of the other length of chain from Step 1. Slide the white travertine drop bead onto a ball head pin. Attach the ball head pin to the end of the extender chain and form a wrapped loop to connect the bead drop.

5 **Bead the middle strand.** Cut two ¾" (1.9cm) lengths of chain and an 8" (21cm) length of beading wire. Use a crimp tube to connect the wire to one end of one ¾" (1.9cm) length of chain. String the following pattern onto the wire: 1 pearl, 1 wavy disc, 1 dagger, and 1 wavy disc. Repeat 6 more times and end with 1 more pearl. Use another crimp tube to connect the end of this bead strand to one end of the other ¾" (1.9cm) length of chain.

6 **Make the top strand.** Slide a pearl onto a ball head pin and form a loop. Repeat to make a total of 5 bead drops. Cut a 3" (7.6cm) length of chain. Attach the loop of a bead drop to the middle link of the chain. Attach bead drops ¼" (0.7cm) and ½" (1.3cm) to the right and left of the middle bead drop.

7 **Assemble the necklace.** Lay the middle strand from Step 5 above the bottom strand from Step 2. Lay the top strand from Step 6 above the middle strand. Measure ½" (1.3cm) up from the 4mm jump rings on each side of the main chain from Step 1. Use a 4mm jump ring on each side to connect the ends of the middle and top strands to the main chain at the ½" (1.3cm) point.

SHOPPING LIST

- 22 - 5 x 16mm travertine dagger drop beads (rose)
- 1 - 5 x 8mm faceted travertine drop bead (white)
- 44 - 2 x 6mm pewter wavy disc beads (brass)
- 29 - 4mm glass round beads (dark rose pearl)
- 18" (46cm) - 1.8mm cable chain (antique gold)
- 20" (52cm) - Beading wire (gold)
- 4 - Crimp tubes (antique gold)
- 1 - 2" (5cm) extender chain (antique gold)
- 6 - 1" (2.5cm) ball head pins (antique gold)
- 5 - 4mm jump rings (antique gold)
- 1 - 6mm jump ring (antique gold)
- 1 - Lobster clasp (antique gold)

TOOLS

- Needle-nose pliers
- Round-nose pliers
- Crimping pliers
- Wire cutters

TECHNIQUES

- Opening and Closing Jump Rings
- Attaching Crimp Tubes/Beads
- Cutting Chain
- Forming a Loop
- Forming a Wrapped Loop

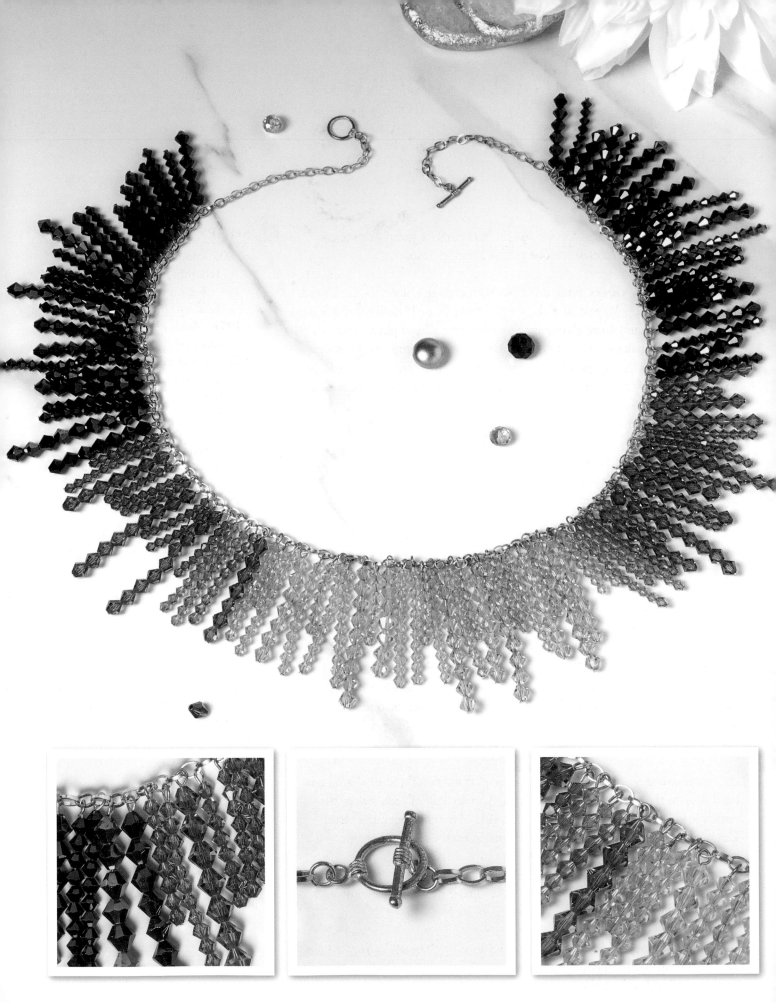

Beaded Stalactite Necklace

Level:
◆ ◆ ◆

Time:
◆ ◆ ◆

The neutral color scheme of this necklace is chic and classic, while the varying lengths of the bead drops give it a funky flair. Pair it with a V-neck top to create a fringe-like effect along the collar. Make 6 extra bead drops, 2 in each color, and attach one set of colors each to a pair of earring wires for a matching set.

1 *Prepare the chain.* Cut a 23" (59cm) length of chain. Use jump rings to connect each end of the chain to one half of a toggle clasp.

2 *Make the champagne drops.* Slide seven 4mm champagne bicones onto a head pin and form a loop. Repeat to make a total of ten 4mm 1" (2.5cm) champagne bead drops. Slide ten 4mm champagne bicones onto a head pin and form a loop. Repeat to make a total of ten 4mm 1½" (3.8cm) champagne bead drops. Slide seven 6mm champagne bicones onto a head pin and form a loop. Repeat to make a total of five 6mm 1½" (3.8cm) champagne bead drops. Slide nine 6mm bicones onto a head pin and form a loop. Repeat to make a total of four 6mm 2" (5cm) champagne bead drops.

3 *Make the smoke drops.* Slide seven 4mm smoke bicones onto a head pin and form a loop. Repeat to make a total of nine 4mm 1" (2.5cm) smoke bead drops. Slide ten 4mm smoke bicones onto a head pin and form a loop. Repeat to make a total of thirteen 4mm 1½" (3.8cm) smoke bead drops. Slide seven 6mm bicones onto a head pin and form a loop. Repeat to make a total of eight 6mm 1½" (3.8cm) smoke bead drops. Slide nine 6mm bicones onto a head pin and form a loop. Repeat to make a total of four 6mm 2" (5cm) smoke bead drops.

4 *Make the black drops.* Slide seven 4mm black bicones onto a head pin and form a loop. Repeat to make a total of seven 4mm 1" (2.5cm) black bead drops. Slide ten 4mm bicones onto a head pin and form a loop. Repeat to make a total of twenty 4mm 1½" (3.8cm) black bead drops. Slide six 6mm black bicones onto a head pin and form a loop. Repeat to make a total of fourteen 6mm 1½" (3.8cm) black bead drops. Slide nine 6mm black bicones onto a head pin and form a loop. Repeat to make a total of seven 6mm 2" (5cm) black bead drops.

5 *Attach the champagne drops.* Connect the loop of a 6mm 2" (5cm) champagne bead drop to the middle loop of the chain. Arrange half of each size of the remaining champagne bead drops on each side of the middle of the chain. Connect the bead drops to consecutive links on each side of the chain.

6 *Attach the smoke drops.* Arrange half of each size of smoke bead drops on the left and right sides of the champagne bead drops. Connect the bead drops to consecutive links on each side of the chain.

7 *Attach the black drops.* Arrange half of each size of black bead drops on the left and right sides of the smoke bead drops. Connect the bead drops to consecutive links on each side of the chain.

SHOPPING LIST

- 180+ - 4mm glass bicone beads (champagne)
- 75+ - 6mm glass bicone beads (champagne)
- 195+ - 4mm glass bicone beads (smoke)
- 95+ - 6mm glass bicone beads (smoke)
- 250+ - 4mm glass bicone beads (black)
- 150+ - 6mm glass bicone beads (black)
- 23" (59cm) - 3.5 x 5mm cable chain (gold)
- 115+ - 2½" (6.5cm) head pins (gold)
- 2 - 4mm jump rings (gold)
- 1 - Toggle clasp set (gold)

TOOLS

- Needle-nose pliers
- Round-nose pliers
- Wire cutters

TECHNIQUES

- Opening and Closing Jump Rings
- Cutting Chain
- Forming a Loop

Beaded Collar Necklace Set

This necklace has a vintage look with a touch of Elizabethan style. Keep the colors of your outfit light to let the deep, rich colors of this design stand out. Pair it with other gold or petrified wood accessories. And you can make matching earrings in just two minutes!

NECKLACE

1 *Prepare the wires.* Cut three 24" (61cm) lengths of beading wire. Use crimp beads to connect one end of each wire to the loops on one half of the clasp set.

2 *String the first section.* String the following onto each of the 3 wires: 1 gold round, 1 chocolate round, and 1 gold round. Thread each wire through a hole in a 3-hole spacer.

3 *String the second section.* String the following onto the inside wire: 1 gold round, 1 chocolate round, and 1 gold round. String the following onto the middle wire: 1 chocolate round, 1 gold round, and 1 chocolate round. String the following onto the outside wire: 3 chocolate rounds. Thread each wire through a hole in a 3-hole spacer.

4 *String the third section.* String the following onto the inside wire: 1 gold round, 6 bicones, and 1 gold round. String the following onto the middle wire: 1 chocolate round, 1 rectangle bead, and 1 chocolate round. String the following onto the outside wire: 1 chocolate round, 8 bicones, and 1 chocolate round. Thread each wire through a hole in a 3-hole spacer.

5 *Repeat.* Repeat Steps 3–4, in order, 4 more times.

6 *Finish beading.* Repeat Step 3, then repeat Step 2.

7 *Finish the necklace.* Use crimp beads to connect the end of each wire to the loops on the other half of the clasp set.

EARRINGS

1 *Make the bead drops.* Slide 1 chocolate round, 1 rectangle bead, and 1 gold round onto a head pin and form a loop to make a bead drop. Repeat to make a second matching bead drop.

2 *Attach the earring wires.* Attach the loop of each bead drop to a separate earring wire.

SHOPPING LIST

- 64 - 8mm round beads (chocolate moss)
- 70 - 4mm glass bicone beads (mirror gold/purple)
- 42 - 4mm round beads (gold)
- 7 - 18 x 25mm petrified wood rectangle beads (brown)
- 12 - 26 x 9mm 3-hole decorative spacers (gold)
- 72" (185cm) - Beading wire (gold)
- 6 - Crimp beads (gold)
- 2 - 2" (5cm) head pins (gold)
- 1 - 18mm 3-strand rod clasp set with extender chain (gold)
- 2 - Earring wires (gold)

TOOLS

- Round-nose pliers
- Crimping pliers
- Wire cutters

TECHNIQUES

- Attaching Crimp Tubes/Beads
- Forming a Loop

Sienna Gold Necklace

This design has a little bit of everything: a touch of tribal style, sparkly beads, strong wire components, and bold color. Use it to dress up a simple cream or white dress, or pair it with a bold pattern. Accessorize with additional pops of orange to highlight the color in the necklace.

1 *Make the mesh strands.* Cut three 6½" (16.5cm) lengths of mesh tubing. Twist one end of each tube like a twist tie and trim the end. Fill each length of mesh tube with copper seed beads. Twist the other end of each tube closed and trim any excess mesh. Bend the eye of an eye pin at a 90-degree angle. Thread it through the inside of a small cord end, out the hole on the end, and form a loop. Repeat with the other small cord end. Bend the eye of an eye pin at a 90-degree angle. Thread the eye pin through the inside of a large gold cord end, out the hole on the end, and form a wrapped loop. Repeat with the other large cord end. Place glue inside both small cord ends and push one end of a filled mesh tube into each cord end. Allow to dry. Place glue inside both large cord ends and push one end of two filled mesh tubes inside each cord end. Allow to dry.

2 *Start the center strands.* Cut a 6½" (16.5cm) and an 8" (20cm) length of beading wire. Place the shorter strand above the longer strand. Use a crimp tube to join one end of both beading wires together and connect the ends to a 6mm jump ring. String 1 rondelle onto both wires together.

3 *Bead the top center strand.* On the top length of wire, string on the following: 1 goldstone oval, 1 rondelle, 1 picture jasper round, the top hole of a 2-strand spacer, 1 goldstone oval, 1 rondelle, the top hole of a 2-strand spacer, 1 rondelle, 1 goldstone oval, the top hole of a 2-strand spacer, 1 picture jasper round, 1 rondelle, and 1 goldstone oval.

4 *Bead the bottom center strand.* On the bottom length of wire, string on the following: 1 copper seed bead, 1 goldstone oval, 1 rondelle, 1 picture jasper round, the bottom hole of the first 2-strand spacer from Step 3, 1 rondelle, 1 goldstone oval, 1 rondelle, the bottom hole of the next 2-strand spacer, 1 rondelle, 1 goldstone oval, 1 rondelle, the bottom hole of the last 2-strand spacer, 1 picture jasper round, 1 rondelle, 1 goldstone oval, and 1 copper seed bead.

5 *Finish the center strands.* Bring the ends of the beading wires from Steps 2–3 together and string 1 rondelle onto both joined wires together. Use a crimp tube to connect each end of joined wires to a 6mm jump ring.

6 *String the bottom strand.* Slide a copper seed bead and an orange octagon onto a head pin and form a loop. Repeat to make a total of 3 bead drops. Cut one 12" (31cm) length of beading wire and string on the following: 2 yellow rounds, 1 bead cap, 3 nuggets, 1 bead cap, 1 yellow round, 1 bead

SHOPPING LIST

- 3 - 20 x 25mm faceted gemstone octagons (orange)
- 10 - 18 x 8mm gemstone nugget beads (orange/cream)
- 3 - 30 x 10mm 2-strand spacers (gold/crystal)
- 8 - 10 x 9mm flat goldstone oval beads (gold glitter)
- 12 - 8mm rondelle beads (mirror gold/gray)
- 4 - 10mm picture jasper gemstone round beads (brown)
- 10 - 4mm gemstone round beads (yellow)
- 800+ - 11/0 seed beads (copper)
- 8 - 10mm flower bead caps (gold)
- 30" (76cm) - 3 x 4mm cable chain (gold)
- 28" (71cm) - Beading wire (gold)
- 20" (51cm) - 5mm open mesh tubing (gold)
- 2 - 10mm open cord ends (gold)
- 2 - 5mm open cord ends (gold)
- 4 - Crimp tubes (gold)
- 3 - 2" (5cm) head pins (gold)
- 4 - 2" (5cm) eye pins (gold)
- 14 - 4mm jump rings (gold)
- 2 - 6mm jump rings (gold)
- 1 - 29mm toggle clasp set (gold/black)

TOOLS

- Needle-nose pliers
- Round-nose pliers
- Crimping pliers
- Wire cutters
- E-6000® glue

TECHNIQUES

- Opening and Closing Jump Rings
- Attaching Crimp Tubes/Beads
- Cutting Chain
- Forming a Loop
- Forming a Wrapped Loop

drop, 1 yellow round, 1 bead cap, 2 nuggets, 1 bead cap, 1 yellow round, 1 bead drop, 1 yellow round, 1 bead cap, 2 nuggets, 1 bead cap, 1 yellow round, 1 bead drop, 1 yellow round, 1 bead cap, 3 nuggets, 1 bead cap, and 2 yellow rounds.

7 *Assemble the necklace.* Open the 6mm jump rings on each end of the center strands from Step 5. Slide the loop from each side of the single mesh tube from Step 1 onto the 6mm jump rings so the tube sits above the center strands. Connect five 4mm jump rings together to make a jump ring chain. Repeat to make another jump ring chain. Connect one end of each jump ring chain to the wrapped loops on each side of the double mesh tubes from Step 1. Connect the other end of each jump ring chain to the 6mm jump rings so the double tubes sit below the center strands. Use crimp tubes to connect each end of the bottom strand from Step 6 to the 6mm jump rings so the strand sits below the double mesh tubes.

8 *Add the chain.* Cut two 15" (38cm) lengths of chain. Use 4mm jump rings to connect the middle link of each chain to one half of a toggle clasp. Use 4mm jump rings to connect the two ends of each chain to the 6mm jump rings from Step 7.

GLOSSARY

Here are a few more miscellaneous terms you might encounter in the Shopping Lists in this book and in the jewelry aisles at your local craft store. For the definitions of most other tools and materials mentioned in this book, see pages 10–13.

Miscellaneous Terms

AB: standing for "aurora borealis," a type of bead finish applied to one side of the bead that reflects different iridescent colors.

druzy crystal: a stone with many tiny, fine crystals on top of a colorful mineral. They are very sparkly and colorful.

extender chain: a short length of chain used at the clasp to make the size of a jewelry piece flexible.

lariat: a necklace style that has a long, straight drop coming from the middle of the necklace. This type of necklace usually does not have a clasp.

Key Types of Chain

cable chain: chain that has interlocking links that are either round or oval in shape.

curb chain: chain that has interlocking links that are semi-curved and seem to interlock on an angle, allowing the chain to lie flat.

flat-link chain: any chain that has interlocking links where each link is somewhat flattened on its sides.

double-link chain: any chain that has two links paired up in place of single links.

drawn cable chain: cable chain with links that are stretched/elongated.

rope chain: chain that has multiple layers of links connected in a spiral-esque pattern, creating a rope effect.

figure-8 chain: chain that has figure-8 shaped links.

Features of Key Materials for Beads/Pendants

glass: very widely available, cheap to expensive, many different cuts and shapes.

crystal: widely available, cheap to expensive.

acrylic: widely available, affordable.

resin: less widely available, affordable.

gemstone: widely available, affordable to expensive, heavy weight.

INDEX

Note: Page numbers in *italics* indicate projects.